How To Ride A Motorcycle SAFELY

Don Candy

No part of this material may be reproduced in any form without express written permission from the author and/or publisher .

No representation is expressed or implied, with regard to accuracy of the information contained in this work and no legal responsibility can be accepted for omissions and/or errors.

Copyright © 2015 by Donald W Candy

All rights reserved.

ISBN 978-0-9964409-5-0

Table of Contents

Chapter One   Why would anyone want to ride a motorcycle

Chapter Two   Equipment

Chapter Three   Defensive driving on two wheels

Chapter Four   Weather

Chapter Five   Dynamics

Chapter Six   Anatomical concerns

Chapter Seven   Psychological concerns

Chapter Eight   Riding together

Chapter Nine   Maintenance

Chapter Ten   Putting it all together

Author's Notes and Disclaimer

The following work is the product of the author's motorcycle riding experience over the past fifty plus years. It is his intent to bring to the reader an enhanced understanding of motorcycle safety, specifically focused on safe riding. Some of the principles involved in safe motorcycle riding require mastering techniques that can be counter-intuitive to some people. These principles and the tried and true techniques for implementing them exist in the public domain. The author has simply used them to support his thesis on safe motorcycle riding.

Chapter One

WHY WOULD ANYONE WANT TO RIDE A MOTORCYCLE?

The only really good reason is it's a fun, economical alternative method of transportation that appeals to the American free spirit. Whether you're on a two thousand mile road trip or just riding around the block after an oil change, it's just plain fun. For those who treasure freedom, riding is a quick cure for life's everyday stresses.

Some think of biking as a male thing – but I gotta tell you there are many, many women out there riding motorcycles. There are clubs just for women and clubs for couples riding separately and clubs for couples riding together. Most clubs don't care who rides with who or how. The good thing about clubs is that they stress safety, riding etiquette and group riding skills. In addition, most have members who are seasoned riders and can help dispel some of the myths about riding motorcycles and offer guidance to new riders.

Whether you're a loan wolf or ride in packs; whether you're male or female; you ride because you like to – it's a kind of freedom thing that reaches way down into the soul of who you are.

So, why not take a little time to learn how to ride safely. There are several misconceptions about safe riding that are usually explained during a motorcycle training program, whether a formal course or self taught, but sometimes not understood by the student to the level required for true safe riding. I'll nail some of the important ones down in the following chapters. I'm going to move past a lot of the 'how to ride' part and concentrate on 'how to ride <u>safely</u>'. The premise here is that the reader/rider has a fundamental understanding of his/her motorcycle and how to ride it.

Chapter Two

EQUIPMENT

Part of riding safely is being prepared for the unexpected. Most bike riders entertain a myth regarding safety. It goes like this: "If I learn to ride safely, the odds of my being involved in an accident are so remote that I shouldn't have to worry about things like proper clothing, gloves, boots or a helmet".

Not True! I witnessed an accident involving a police officer who was blocking an intersection for a funeral motorcade. A lady coming out of a service station pulled around a stopped car on the crossing road that was blocking her view of the officer and accelerated right into him and his motorcycle. He suffered a broken right leg and a broken left collar bone. I was surprised he lived. He was thrown almost twenty feet and his motorcycle was totaled. Had he not been wearing the appropriate safety gear he could have (probably would have) easily been killed or permanently disabled. Riding a motorcycle without proper safety gear is like riding in a car without a seat belt - when the unexpected happens your odds of being seriously hurt or killed are dramatically increased.

Not a block from my home a neighbor had pulled his motorcycle over to the side of the road and stopped to talk to a friend when a teenager who had just gotten her drivers license pulled out of an alley, lost control of her car and hit the motorcycle and driver. He died at the scene. He was wearing jeans and a T-shirt – no helmet.

Our streets are littered with reckless, careless and inexperienced drivers. Motorcyclists are not immune to encounters with these people, who are in reality, 'accidents looking for a place to happen'. And, unfortunately, some of 'these people' are on motorcycles. Don't become a statistic. Pay attention to safety; before, during and after you ride. Buy and use the best safety gear you can find.

CHAPTER THREE

DEFENSIVE DRIVING ON TWO WHEELS

I started to name this chapter 'Defensive Driving on Steroids' because that's what it takes to survive on a motorcycle. Not everyone driving an automobile is an inexperienced, reckless, careless, idiot, moron – but some are and we'll call them doofuses (Google that), ready to put you in a hurt locker without blinking an eye.

So, I survived my hundred or so thousand miles on motorcycles by assuming that all automobile, truck and bus drivers and unfortunately a growing number of surviving motorcyclists fit one or more of these doofus categories. And looking back over the years, many of them didn't disappoint me. Let's look at defensive driving in traffic first and then we'll look at intersections.

When riding in traffic a motorcyclist should use his/her defensive driving skills (hopefully) learned over his/her years of experience driving a car, modified for additional 'stuff that happens' pertaining specifically to motorcycle riders. If you are not already a defensive driver either don't buy a motorcycle, sell your motorcycle if you already have one or put it in storage until you become competent in driving defensively – then learn those added skills needed for riding a motorcycle. The most important mind set a motorcyclist can burn into his/her read-only memory is that of his/her *extreme vulnerability to the acts of others* – acts that masquerade themselves as sometimes being predictable, and sometimes not so much.

Defensive driving starts with actions of the driver. Obey *all* traffic laws and regulations. Use your turn signals *any time* you intend to move from your current driving status – all turns, all lane changes and your emergency blinkers when stopped on the side of the road. Always let other drivers know your intentions.

In traffic, use the same rules for spacing as you would in a car; one car length per ten miles per hour. Don't reduce your spacing to a motorcycle length. On a two lane road drive at or below the speed limit in the center of the lane and maintain separation. Always keep in mind an emergency escape route and plan. If you see a vehicle parked at the side of the road ahead, you need to be thinking about what to do, where to go, and how to execute your emergency escape if that vehicle or something blocked to your vision near that vehicle presents a problem. Likewise with a vehicle stopped at a crossing road – what do you do, where do you go, how do you stop, who's behind you, how do you react if they move into your path? This is what I call dynamic situational awareness. You need to adjust your situational awareness and emergency escape plan as you drive. This awareness combined with the other requirements for driving should become your primary thought process while riding a motorcycle, leaving you time to think about nothing else.

Now expand the road to a three or four lane highway.

HOW TO RIDE A MOTORCYCLE SAFELY

What changes? I prefer to ride in the outside lane (the lane closest to the curb or shoulder) and position myself between two vehicles in the lane next to me. It's not that I don't trust those drivers, it's just that I don't trust any other driver. If I ride next to (right beside) a car there is a very real possibility that the driver is a certified doofus and might look, but not see me, before he pulls into my lane and runs me off the road. When I ride between cars I can see their signals (if they use them) if they decide to move into my lane. If they don't see me or use their signals then they pull into a space that I have reserved for doofuses. The only other lane I ride in is the center lane in preparation for a left turn. The good news here is; on highways with three or more lanes in each direction most, if not all, exits are to the right – my favorite lane. When I do have to shift lanes, however, I begin from my position between the vehicles to my left using my turn signals. Most drivers are good courteous people and show additional courtesy to bikers, so I wait for the driver to my left rear to acknowledge my intent by falling back slightly. Then I move into his lane and position myself between two vehicles in the lane to my left and repeat this process until I reach the center lane.

By riding in the right lane I might lose five miles per hour because I'm not in the "fast lane", but hey, it's a small price to pay for peace of mind. I always travel at the same speed as the two cars to my left. If the car to my front left signals right, I back off , let him pull into my lane ahead of me and re-adjust my position relative to the two cars to my left.

And then there's the motorcycle at an intersection – one of the most dangerous places to be. For example; you're at a stop sign on a small road that ends at a T with a two lane highway. A car comes around a curve on the highway to your left and engages his right turn signal to signify that he intends to turn right into the road you're on. So, it's okay to pull out in front of him since he has been kind enough to let you know of his intentions – right? Not at all. There are people (in one or more of the categories above) that don't see motorcycles. There is a possibility that this driver is looking for the right road to turn into to get where he or she is going and might be focused on the street sign which only becomes readable as the car gets closer to the intersection. As the driver gets close enough to read the sign and discovers it's the wrong street what does he/she do? You guessed it – he/she accelerates to regain the speed lost while concentrating on the sign and wonders where the motorcycle he/she is about to flatten came from. Car-1, motorcycle-0. Stuff like this happens more often than you might think.

When you come to an intersection, whether a two, three or four way stop, obey the right of way laws but be sure of the intentions of others stopped at the intersection before you exercise your right to move into harm's way. There's a good chance that there will be a doofus present representing one or more of the aforementioned categories ready to do you in if you're not on your toes.

You're at a stoplight and it's red. It's one of those lights that turns green every fifteen minutes whether it needs to or not and the guy behind you has crept to within six inches of your tail light. You're turning left from a small road that Ts into a busy highway where the speed limit is 45 mph and most people are coming off the hill to your left doing 60+. The cross light turns yellow and the traffic speeds up to get through the intersection before it turns red. Your light turns green and a microsecond later the guy behind you starts honking – you're surrounded by doofuses; sometimes they come in packs. Hold your ground! You've got to be

HOW TO RIDE A MOTORCYCLE SAFELY

damned sure everybody's going to stop before you go. At least one of the farthest from the light and fastest moving drivers is more interested in making the light than letting you live. Don't move until all cross traffic has either run the red light or is obviously trying to stop before doing so and in your judgment they have room to stop and they will be able to do so. Oh, and give the guy honking behind you a loving gesture that is deserving of his obnoxiousness.

There are hundreds of other examples I could expound upon here but I think you should be getting the point I'm trying to make: When riding a motorcycle, you and *only you* are responsible for your safety. There are no seat belts or airbags but there are doofuses aplenty and they'll get you if you let them.

Before we leave this subject I should mention that at the other end of the spectrum form the doofuses are the drivers that respect motorcyclists and go out of their way to show that respect by yielding to them, sometimes to a fault. I wish I had a nickel (make that a dollar) for every time I've stopped at an intersection at which a car that was clearly already stopped and was intending to either turn or cross my intended path and had the right of way, insisted on yielding to me. I sit there waiting for him/her to move on through because he/she clearly has the right of way. I'm thinking, 'maybe I should go ahead and go'. The driver's thinking. 'that poor guy's on a motorcycle. Some day he's going to die – but not now, not today. I'm not going to be the one to kill him – we'll be here all day before I move'. This is a person who is afraid of motorcycles; motorcycles (not cars) kill people and he also probably thinks guns (not people) cause violence. The important thing here is to realize that these folks have your safety at heart and you need to respect their intent and let them win the contest. Always use eye contact to be sure of the other drivers intent. Usually they'll give you a hand signal to proceed. But be extra careful when more than one other vehicle is stopped at the intersection – things can become confused when you're trying to figure out who is and who is not going to obey the law.

CHAPTER FOUR

WEATHER

If your motorcycle is your primary transportation vehicle you're going to get wet. There are some pretty good sets of rain gear out there that when combined with a water tight full faced helmet will give you moderate protection in sub-hurricane conditions. The issue of safety on wet roads raises its ugly head though. And it can get pretty ugly. If you didn't have to accelerate, brake or turn in the rain you'd be in pretty good shape except for the increase in danger from motorists who don't know how to drive in bad weather. Let's take this stuff one thing at a time.

Rain is more dangerous for the motorcyclist and automobile drivers at the beginning of the shower because the water floats the oils from the road surface and produces a slippery ride. It's best to avoid this problem by not riding during this period – usually about ten minutes in a downpour to about thirty minutes in a light rain shower. If you have to ride during this period be extremely careful. Once you're past this period and all of the road oils are washed down the storm drain your tires ought to give you the traction needed for cautious driving – no hard turns, braking or acceleration. As most other traffic does in a rain shower, slow down and exercise caution. Visibility issues will increase with the magnitude of the rainfall – you don't have windshield wipers on your helmet visor. Put your defensive driving technique on steroids – strange things happen in the rain.

Okay, you can handle the rain if you have to. What about ice and snow? Simple. Keep your bike in the garage and take your four wheel drive SUV. If you don't have one of those take a bus or train if they're running. Ice, snow and motorcycles don't mix. Period.

Wind can be a problem for lighter bikes. If the wind gusts begin causing the bike to lean enough to initiate a turn then turn around and go back home. Generally, when the bike is upward of about seven hundred pounds it takes a lot of wind to affect safety, but then sometimes you'll run into a lot of wind. Use your judgment – stay safe.

Heat is only a problem because those damned motorcycle air conditioners don't work in the summer and the motor heat adds to the problem. If you can't take the heat stay out of the . . . Extreme cold calls for the same solution.

CHAPTER FIVE

DYNAMICS

To understand what's going on when you ride a motorcycle you need to have knowledge of the dynamics involved in a moving two wheeled vehicle. Not as difficult as you might think, but probably not as simple either.

Try this; on a level surface with the kickstand down, move your bike to the upright position with the front wheel pointing dead ahead. Now without touching the handlebars, let the bike rest back on the kickstand using your legs. With a heavy bike be ready to assist with the handlebars. Either way, the wheel will turn toward the side that the kickstand is on, which is the side you leaned it toward (usually the left side on American motorcycles). This is good! This is how your bike is designed. This characteristic, however, can be confusing when riding at speeds above ten to twenty miles per hour. This characteristic leads your conscious mind to believe that at driving speed if you turn the handlebars to the left you will turn left just like you do in a car. THIS IS NOT TRUE!

Think about it. When you turn the handlebars to the left – what happens? The bike leans to the right due to centrifugal force and it will therefore turn to the right. All tandem two wheel vehicles turn in the direction they are leaning. The harder you turn left the tighter the bike will turn to the right. We'll dig into this further in chapter seven. For now let's just agree that we all understand the first principle of 'counter-steering', ie; at speeds above ten to twenty miles per hour when we turn the handlebars slightly to the left our bike goes to the right, and of course, vice-versa. Once again this is called *counter-steering.* This is what your mind learned long ago when you figured out how to ride a bicycle but you had no clue how you learned it– *muscle-memory!*

I've known some folks who have ridden motorcycles for years and argue that it is the fact that they lean to one side and that makes the bike turn in the direction they are leaning. So, they claim, it's their leaning that makes them turn, not this fantasy called counter-steering. So, I say to them, try this; on a deserted straight road, without leaning at all, momentarily put slight forward pressure on the left handlebar as if you wanted to make a gentle turn to the right. Which way does the bike turn? *Not to the right!* It turns to the left – and you *didn't lean!* Wow, what a concept. This is called, once again, counter-steering. The folks that don't understand this usually haven't had formal motorcycle training.

It should be noted that counter-steering doesn't require physically turning the handlebars. All that is required is enough pressure on the handlebars toward the opposite direction of the turn to maintain the lean of the motorcycle and rider required for the turn. More pressure increases the lean which tightens the turn. Less pressure decreases the lean and reduces the rate of turn. To roll out of the turn use pressure in the opposite direction.

HOW TO RIDE A MOTORCYCLE SAFELY

Fact is, when riding a street motorcycle the rider shouldn't lean at all relative to the bike - and you should convince your passenger, when you have one, not to lean as well. Keeping the combined center-of-gravity (rider, passenger and bike) in the same plane as the rear wheel allows the tires on a street bike to perform as they were designed to perform and keeps rider and passenger in a constant comfortable position. This is especially important on wet roads.

At slow speeds counter-steering yields to what I call conventional steering and the rider finds him/herself making the bike turn in the same direction as the handlebars move. But to make the conventional turn at slow speed he/she must first make a small counter-steer to put the combined center-of-gravity on the same side of the bike as the turn. When you see a little kid learning to ride a bicycle and it looks like he/she is wandering all over the sidewalk, that little kid's brain is developing the muscle-memory necessary to ride a bike – this includes both steering and counter-steering and when to use which. This is the stage of life when most people learn about steering and counter-steering – when learning to ride a bicycle as a child. They have no clue as to what's going on – they just learn what works and viola, they can ride! Once again, more on this in chapter seven where we'll define muscle-memory and discuss the importance of understanding the potential conflict between muscle-memory and conscious habits.

What about braking? How do you stop a motorcycle safely? We'll divide this subject into two sections; normal braking and emergency braking.

Bringing a motorcycle to a stop isn't rocket science, but there are a few things we need to know about doing it safely. Just like a car, when you apply your brakes on a motorcycle the front wheel receives most of the bike's weight. The friction of the braking force causes the combined center of gravity to move forward. That, of course, means that the rear wheel will have a lighter load and therefore tend to lock up before the front if you apply equal braking force (as many people incorrectly believe is the correct procedure) to both. To remedy that problem you should apply more braking force to the front wheel. Depending on the bike, the range is generally 70/30 plus or minus five percent front/back. A light bike (~300-600 pounds) will require more front braking than a heavy one (~600-1100 pounds) because the rider's weight and higher center of gravity will have more influence on the front to rear weight ratio of the light bike.

Emergency stopping should be avoided. "How", you ask, "do you go about avoiding emergencies?" Simple - practice defensive riding. I've been riding for over fifty years and I've never had to make what I consider an emergency stop. "And what do you consider an emergency stop?" you ask. My definition of an emergency stop is one where a collision is eminent and the rider must take drastic emergency action to minimize injury to him/her self. Knowing when that condition exists is a primary issue and what to do when it does is an issue of equal importance. Also, emergency action does *not* mean intentionally ditching your bike, losing half a pound of skin and breaking a bunch of bones. You should be able to depend on your defensive driving skills and your driving skills to stay safe on your bike, that is to keep you from ever allowing an emergency situation to arise.

However, your motorcycle will stop in an amazingly short distance if you know the procedure and how to

HOW TO RIDE A MOTORCYCLE SAFELY

execute it properly. Read up on the science of stopping a motorcycle and avoiding collisions. It involves smooth continuous application of force on the front brake while simultaneously removing pressure on the rear break as your combined weight moves forward. The procedure is unique for each make/model/rider combination. The only way to perfect the procedure is through practice. When you learn how to develop the procedure to fit your configuration find a parking lot and practice with a friend. Then sharpen your defensive skills so you won't ever need to use it.

CHAPTER SIX

ANATOMICAL CONCERNS

There are many types of motorcycles; cruising, sport, track racing, off-road racing, dirt bikes. . . There are one cylinder, two, three and four cylinder and even six and eight cylinder bikes. Prices run from ~$2,000 to more than $50,000. When in the market for a new or used motorcycle there are many things to consider. Of these, in my opinion, safety and comfort are the most important. I certainly can't speak for all classes of riders so I'll just cover my preferences from my street bike experience and stress safety.

I like the medium weight street bikes. This class runs from about 600 to 850 pounds and is adequate for road trips as well as errands or pleasure riding and is still fairly economical to maintain and operate. This class of bike is usually designed and configured for both comfort and safety. Acceleration and braking are typically better than the larger street bikes but this class is usually not as maneuverable as some of the smaller bikes.

HOW TO RIDE A MOTORCYCLE SAFELY

Configuration and safety are closely related. Racing configurations suffer in safety when ridden in traffic on the streets. Conversely, street bikes suffer in safety when raced or ridden off-road. Bottom line, decide which configuration you want for your bike and be safe by always riding it *only* as it was designed to be ridden. Street motorcycles put the rider in an upright position with arms comfortably extended to well placed handlebars. The foot pegs or floorboards are positioned forward in a comfortable, foot slightly forward position. Many motorcycle manufacturers offer similar models with slight differences in height and configuration to accommodate different sized riders. This is good. Uncomfortable bikes ridden in a mode for which they were not designed and/or not configured to your body are unsafe – be sure you address this safety requirement carefully when acquiring your motorcycle.

CHAPTER SEVEN

PSYCHOLOGICAL CONCERNS

One day when you were around a year old, crawling around on the floor, your little mind thought, "why am I crawling when everyone else is walking?" So, you made an early life decision to learn to walk. First you had to learn to stand. "Ah, that was pretty easy, now lets tackle the walking thing!" Not so easy – lots of trial and error. The first thing you do is learn to fall gracefully - usually right on your butt because that's what causes the least amount of pain. After a few days you graduate to the toddler stage and you've been walking the rest of your life.

You're around one year old – are you thinking about what you're doing? No, you just want to walk like the big people and you're highly motivated. What's actually happening here is that sub-conscientiously you are training your brain to coordinate your muscles to achieve your highly motivated goal – walking. In the human brain, just above the level of involuntary muscle movement like heartbeat, breathing and eye focusing, lies a level of brain activity that allows your body to learn to do things not required for basic life - but this process still remains below the level of conscious thought. In other words you're learning but you may not have a clue as to what or how. I'm not sure what psychologists call this but I and others call it muscle-memory.

Practice makes perfect – right? What practice really does is develop muscle-memory, and the more you practice the better developed your muscle-memory becomes. Athletic coaches, special forces operators, police officers, sailing and flight instructors all understand muscle-memory the and importance of practice to keep it finely tuned.

Fast-forward a bit and now you're five years old and your parents buy you a bicycle for Christmas – with training wheels. You say to yourself, "man, this is easy, I turn left – I go left, I turn right – I go right, I pedal forward – I go forward, I pedal backward, I stop. I'm a genius, I've learned to ride! Then comes New Years Day and Dad takes the training wheels off. Not so easy, huh. You are embarking on one of your life's most difficult muscle-memory training missions. But after a few days of having your dad run behind you, holding on at first, and then just trying to grab you when you're about to crash and burn, you wobble yourself halfway down the street before wiping out. Your mother bought you a helmet, and some knee and elbow pads so your pride is the only thing that suffers. A few days later you make it all the way around the block, you're well on your way to becoming a bona fide master bicyclist.

And you should be congratulated! Your brain has developed your sub-conscious muscle-memory to a level of coordination that allows you to pedal, brake, steer and counter-steer, all of which are necessary to ride a bike. Oh, yeah, at the ripe old age of five you don't even know what counter-steering is, do you? Well, at this point in your riding career you don't have a need-to-know – so we'll just keep it a secret. I doubt if your dad even knows what it is anyway.

But! Later in life, as you become more proficient and begin to ride faster and perhaps graduate to a motorcycle, understanding counter-steering will become *very* important. Why? You ask. In chapter four we discussed the mechanics of counter-steering. Here we'll discuss the psychology of it.

I like examples – I don't like this one. Fort Worth Texas a few years back; a police officer recently added to the motorcycle corps while escorting a motorcade had a fatal single vehicle accident. Why did this happen – let's look at it and see if we can figure it out.

The motorcade was traveling down a road that had a lane closed off for maintenance with the accompanying concrete barricade to one side. The officer was riding side by side with another officer (something that I will tell you is unsafe in the next chapter yet routinely done by motorcycle escorts). The officer was between the barricade and his fellow riding officer. They proceeded into a turn. As the turn progressed it became tighter (more curved). Suddenly the officer turned into the wall and was killed. The speed was approximately thirty miles per hour. After a careful post accident investigation of the motorcycle, the road, the barrier and the fellow officer the cause was officially classified as *unknown* and to the best of my knowledge remains so to this day.

So let me tell you what I think happened (actually, I'm pretty sure this is what happened): As the turn tightened the officer who had just ridden with the motorcycle corps for a few weeks found himself pinned between the barricade and his fellow officer riding next to him. The fact that he had only been with the corps for a few weeks doesn't mean he wasn't an experienced

HOW TO RIDE A MOTORCYCLE SAFELY

rider – the conditions here could cause any very seasoned rider to react as this officer did in a situation like this, which was likely a very different mode of riding than he'd been used to. The turn is tightening and the officer found himself in a situation that caused his conscious mind to override his muscle-memory. When drifting toward the concrete barrier while confined by his fellow officer on his other side and suddenly discovering he was in trouble, instead of allowing his sub-conscious muscle-memory to increase the forward force on the inside handlebar to tighten his turn and follow the barricade, he allowed his conscious mind to take control and turned the handlebars in the direction away from the barrier which actually turned him directly into it. Part of any motorcycle rider's problem in a situation like this is that he also drives a car and in a moment where there are many distractions and an emergency reaction is required the conscious mind can very easily override muscle-memory. Had he not been confined and forced to make a quick conscious decision this would not have happened. This was the unfortunate loss of one of our most respected and revered public servants.

Ever wonder why athletes go through slumps – especially pitchers and quarterbacks; *muscle-memory override!* When athletes, who are key members of a team and bear more than their fair share of responsibility for the team's success, have a bad day (throw three interceptions or walk four batters), they are prone to allowing their conscious mind to interfere with the muscle-memory they have acquired over years of practice. In other words they begin over-thinking the problem. On an individual bases, this problem often affects golfers. Coaches who understand this problem can sometimes counter it with proper psychological and encouragement techniques.

I explained counter-steering to a friend of mine once and mentioned the problem of overriding muscle-memory with conscious thought and he said, "yeah, I'll keep that in mind". The next day he told me he was in the middle of a turn when he remembered what I said, got confused and ran off the road. The good news was that he turned into a level field (of corn). This guy had ridden that very bike for ten years. This kind of incident can happen to anyone any time but it's most likely to occur in a tightening turn when we suddenly realize the problem and allow our conscious mind to jump in and screw up a perfectly good day.

So what do we do to prevent muscle-memory override. Simple, we build a strong link between our counter-steering muscle-memory and our conscious mind. Long ago, after experiencing a minor override problem, I began bringing my conscious thought process into each turn I made. After probably forty years I still do that. I use forward pressure on the inside handlebar to make my turns and I do it consciously – every time! If the turn tightens I add a little more pressure – it's that simple.

Try to limit your riding to transportation or pleasure. Don't ride when:

- overly tired
- influenced by alcohol or medication
- in a hurry to get somewhere
- rushing to beat a deadline
- road conditions are bad
- your bike has any safety concerns
- you're having any kind of emotional problem

CHAPTER EIGHT

RIDING TOGETHER

In my neighborhood I often see many (maybe up to a hundred) bicyclists in a group coming down a narrow two lane, hilly, curvy, fairly heavily traveled country road, sometimes four abreast. Texas law limits them to two abreast. In Texas there are bicycle laws but no licensing of bicycles and no test or safety course required to ride one on public streets. So what you see is what you get – lawlessness.

On the other hand, when I see motorcycles traveling together, more often than not they are staggered with a decent separation. And usually there's no more than four or five. This is the way it's supposed to be, but not always what you see.

How should motorcycles ride together? Up to about ten motorcycles can travel together in relative safety if they stagger themselves with a down-road bike length separation at low speed, increasing to two full bike-lengths at highway speeds. As the group approaches a stop it is safe to carefully pull up side-by-side and then separate again while pulling away from the stop. Club organized group rides usually have appointed leaders and trailers riding at the beginning and end of a group with the responsibility of keeping the group together. Some clubs will organize large rides in separate groups of about ten, each with a leader and trailer, sometimes separated by a hundred yards or so.

When riding in groups defensive driving is still important. Even though there is perceived safety in numbers there is always the possibility of running into (or being run into by) an occasional random doofus.

The clubs that I'm familiar with in North Texas stress (and teach) safety. Some have certified motorcycle instructors among their members. So finding and joining a club might be a good idea for new motorcycle owners. I ride with friends occasionally but prefer to ride alone. Is that anti-social or am I just shy?

CHAPTER NINE

MAINTENANCE

If you take your bike to a qualified motorcycle shop for regular inspections and maintenance your safety maintenance-wise is typically in good hands. But you still need to watch for problems between regular maintenance intervals. Some things to keep an eye on are the condition of tires, brakes, battery, lights, wheels and bearings, belts/chains, air and oil filters and leaks of any sort.

Let's start with tires. Motorcycle tires, for the most part, are built as well or better than automobile tires – but they are still subject to road damage, wear and balance problems. It's a good idea to do a pre-ride inspection of the tires and wheels each time you ride. It only takes a minute and it can save you a lot of grief. It's also a good idea to check the air pressure in both tires on a regular basis – I check mine every month or 300 miles, which ever comes first. I do this as part of a regular routine maintenance check – tires, wheels, brakes and belt/chain. Never wear the tires beyond the state inspection tread wear limit which is typically the same as for cars – 1/16 of an inch. This is especially important for street bikes – if (when) you get caught in a shower – and it happens - the first few minutes are the most dangerous because the water brings the road oils to the surface. Oil is lighter than water. That's when you need the most traction and when worn out tires are the most dangerous.

A good motorcycle shop will use a lift that lifts the bike from the center, leaving both wheels able to rotate freely. With this type of lift the mechanic (or technician, as they like to be called these days) can thoroughly inspect the wheels, spokes, tires, brakes and belt or chain and sprockets. This type of lift also provides easy access to the engine for inspection and filter replacement. .

On the other hand if you prefer to do your own maintenance, here are some things to be very careful about:
- Don't attempt to replace your own tires. Motorcycle tires require special equipment to avoid damage to the wheel, insure proper bead seating and balancing – all very important. Take your wheels off the bike and to a motorcycle parts/tire store with a good reputation and have them mount your new tires. Most stores charge only for balancing, not for mounting. Many require wheels only because they don't have facilities for handling motorcycles.
- Buy a motorcycle lift. You can get a good one from one of the Chinese tool stores for about $70 – a good investment because it enables a much better inspection and makes changing tires, belts/chains and oil much, much easier.
- Use the bike manufacturer's recommended brake pads, fluid, and oil/air filters. In other words buy only O.E.M. parts and consumables for your bike.

CHAPTER TEN

PUTTING IT ALL TOGETHER

Is riding a motorcycle dangerous? Only if you let it be!

If you:

- learn and practice safe, defensive riding principles
- understand the dynamics of the vehicle you ride
- assume everyone else is a doofus
- never ride your bike when you're in a hurry or trying to beat a deadline, intoxicated or ill
- always use your turn signals
- always drive with your headlight (s) on
- ride only in good weather when possible
- wear visible clothing
- keep your bike well maintained
- wear the best protective gear you can find
- keep your conscious mind linked to your muscle-memory when turning

You'll be safe.

ABOUT THE AUTHOR

Engineer, commercial pilot, motorcycle enthusiast, flight instructor, sailing instructor, author and retired CEO; I've led a life of adventure. My life experiences and love for motorcycles led to this book. My wife Karan, our son, daughter, four grandchildren and I enjoy traveling, sailing, skiing and water sports.

Printed in Great Britain
by Amazon